CORPUS

CORPUS

Michael Symmons Roberts

CAPE POETRY

Published by Jonathan Cape 2004

2 4 6 8 10 9 7 5 3 1

First published in Great Britain in 2004 by
Jonathan Cape
Random House, 20 Vauxhall Bridge Road, London SW1V 2SA

Random House Australia (Pty) Limited
20 Alfred Street, Milsons Point, Sydney,
New South Wales 2061, Australia

Random House New Zealand Limited
18 Poland Road, Glenfield,
Auckland 10, New Zealand

Random House South Africa (Pty) Limited
Endulini, 5A Jubilee Road, Parktown 2193, South Africa

The Random House Group Limited Reg. No. 954009
www.randomhouse.co.uk

A CIP catalogue record for this book is
available from the British Library

ISBN 0-224-07342-7

Papers used by Random House are natural,
recyclable products made from wood grown in sustainable forests;
the manufacturing processes conform to the environmental
regulations of the country of origin

Typeset by Palimpsest Book Production Limited, Polmont, Stirlingshire
Printed and bound in Great Britain by Biddles Ltd, King's Lynn, Norfolk

for Joseph, Patrick & Griffith

CONTENTS

ACKNOWLEDGEMENTS

Acknowledgements are due to the editors of the following:
Image, Grand Street Poetry (Chicago), *Poetry Daily, Poetry London, Poetry Review, Ploughshares, Quadrant, Southern Review, Stand, The Gift* (Stride), *Sou'wester, Times Literary Supplement, Wild Reckoning.*

'The Gifts' was commissioned for broadcast by BBC Radio 3's 'The Verb'.
'Post-Mortem' was commissioned for broadcast by BBC Radio 3's 'Poetry Proms'.

The writing of this has been greatly assisted by a K. Blundell Trust Award from the Society of Authors.

PELT

I found the world's pelt
nailed to the picture-rail
of a box-room in a cheap hotel.

So that's why rivers dry to scabs,
that's why the grass weeps every dawn,
that's why the wind feels raw:

the earth's an open wound,
and here, its skin hangs
like a trophy, atrophied beyond all

taxidermy, shrunk into a hearth rug.
Who fleeced it?
No record in the guest-book.

No-one paid, just pocketed the blade
and walked, leaving the bed
untouched, TV pleasing itself.

Maybe there was no knife.
Maybe the world shrugs off a hide
each year to grow a fresh one.

That pelt was thick as reindeer,
so black it flashed with blue.
I tried it on, of course, but no.

ASCENSION DAY

In the *Blue Lobster Café* backyard,
the head chef – arms outstretched –
bears what looks like a body,

but conjures six cook's shirts,
hot-laundered, pegged out,
dripping in a drench of sun.

As they dry, their half-hearted
semaphore becomes
more urgent, untranslatable.

Sex and death are in the air
this May morning: pollen and spent
blossom on an aimless breeze;

crab-backs, prawn skins, clams,
black-violet mussel shells,
all reek in sun-baked bin-sacks.

A rare dish is right for those who
have lain bandaged in a tomb for weeks:

quince and quail to demonstrate
that fruit and birds still grow on trees,

eels to show that fish still needle streams.
Rarer still, some blind white crabs,

not bleached but blank, from such
a depth of ocean that the sun would drown

if it approached them. Two-thirds
of the earth is sea; and two-thirds of that sea

– away from currents, coasts and reefs –
is lifeless, colourless, pure weight.

CORPSE

This is my body, me, splayed
on the road's crown like a shot bird.

Back street. No cars. Men step
over me, dogs and crows investigate.

My eyes gape. Circuitry of soul
is broken. I am in an odd shape

– twisted star – a pose I could never
strike in life. Gymnastic, almost.

This double-jointedness in death
soon tightens as the muscles lock.

My face cracks in the sun.
My hands point up and down the street,

as if to say *'I came from here,
and there was where I headed . . .'*

Pregnant with its own ferment,
my gut swells a blue uniform.

I do not recall the battle, army,
cause. I cannot see a bullet-hole.

There is a voice nearby – not loud.
The sky – not bright – is green with storms.

CORPOREALITY

Troops in the desert,
waiting for *GO*. On TV

the General, interviewed.
Behind, one of his men

21, 22, 23, is kissing his own
shadow in the blazing heat.

Press-ups? Get some shade boy!
But he won't, *30, 31,* it keeps

muscles tight, and kills
the boredom. More,

he's hypnotised, rehearsing
death. Each *37,8,9* dip and lift

resolves his shadow, then
dissolves it into him,

the split of soul *43* from body
44 played over and over.

The sun has a dark heart,
dark as in invisible, as

in unseen, unencompassed.
Bodies get in its way,

so it blanks them out.
He's up to *50*, pushing *60*,

General unclips microphone,
nods, walks away.

Couple of retakes, Sir?
When will you cross the desert?

Desert, as in empty,
though it is of course a flood,

an ocean of unbounded light.
And on its further shore

a woman turns fruit on
her market stall to help it ripen.

Her shadow, even when sun
is sieved through bone–

and–mustard coloured
canopies, is spilling over apples,

melons, dates. The day needs her
to stand and break its light,

since pure light is invisible.
Once, a girl, she stared it out

to spite her mother,
and the spiteful sun

gave her a dark print
of its heart in every blink.

ATTEMPTS ON YOUR LIFE

For example, that winter night
which slid from the hills to tap
your soul. It rubbed against you
like a cat in from the cold.
It frisked you gently so as not
to wake you. It believed

your soul was written on a slip
of rice paper, tucked between
your teeth, behind your ear
like a cigarette, or pushed
under your skin like a prayer
into a wall; healed, subsumed.

Of course, the night left empty-handed.
Worse, it swept the streets for litter
as you slept − intact − your soul as
heavy as your self; sleek, seal-like,
made of light, love, marrow,
milk and honey, made of body.

POST-MORTEM

This is my body, me on the slab,
lying in the sun which burns
as if to melt the etched frost
from the man-tall windows.

In this swelter, how can flies
resist the game, the deep red
sweetmeats in the cavern of me,
vascular stamens of a Venus trap?

My three skin-petals gape,
one from each shoulder to waist,
and one up from my chest,
which covers nose and mouth.

She wears a mask too,
a plastic face-shield, gloves,
blue shiny gown; armour of life
against the seeds of where I've been.

She feels ice-spores of marble
in my pulse-less arms.
She pictures, on my tight shut eyes,
the exile's distant glaze.

She heaves huge jars down from a shelf,
unscrews one, lifts my gut-coil
from its marinade of formalin,
gently shakes the drips onto the floor.

She weighs it on a grocer's scales
and slips it into me. It's cold,
but her assistant settles it
and stitches it in place.

Liver, stomach, lungs, each cradled,
slid and sewn; painstaking work.
They lift my sawn ribs like a lid,
plant the heart, and close its cage.

They take out the wood brick
that propped my shoulder-blades
and arched me open. I sink onto
the metal slab as though I'm sighing.

My viscera complete, they fold in
all three petals, seal with thread
the Y-shaped wound.
I am all of a piece, but lifeless.

My skin sticks to the stainless steel.
They hose me down, under and over,
yanking me up with a leg or an arm
to drench me, peel me from the slab.

Water gutters over earth-brown tiles
and chokes into a central drain.
She scissors free my mouth and eyes
from stitched serenity.

She kisses – passionless –
my paper lips
and waits for my first gasp,
then gestures to a mustard-coloured door:

'It has been longer than you think',
she says, 'In the next room you will find
some simple clothes and food. You will
be hungry. Leave us now.'

On that final night, his meal was formal:
lamb with bitter leaves of endive, chervil,
bread with olive oil and jars of wine.

Now on Tiberias' shores he grills
a carp and catfish breakfast on a charcoal fire.
This is not hunger, this is resurrection:

he eats because he can, and wants to
taste the scales, the moist flakes of the sea,
to rub the salt into his wounds.

THE BOX

In case of catastrophe,
winter can be recreated
from this skeleton of leaf.

All the bitter subtleties
of crab apple are tangled
here, as is the DNA

of dew-point, calibration
of the second when a tree
lets go, the recipe for clouds

on the horizon like a new
born mountain range,
like north itself.

And with the leaf,
this relic box contains
a hair curl from a child

to reconstruct humanity,
though all the lights and currents
of his soul are lost to us.

Spores, antennae, claws,
the box will hold all evolution.
It will be full and empty.

The cook said: *'Let this be a feast*
for those who hungered all their lives.'

So the skinny ones stripped the sow,
and found stretched out inside her
– like her soul, like her self – a lamb,
with its head in the place of her heart,
with its hind legs tucked to leap.

Generations back, a hoard of peaches,
apricots and plums was laid down
for the day of resurrection; treats for all
those dry tongues, soil-caked palates.

Fruit was picked, clad, crated,
shelved in beech sheds.
Doors were sealed with wax, padlocked
and left. Children's children waited.

In the sheds, each fruit still lies
cocooned in careful shrouds of vine-leaves,
tissue, moss. Each is now a dark, sweet
twist of gum, as sharp as scent.

Outside, stripped trees as light as balsa
ring the sheds and knit into each others
roots to stand. Mosquitoes cloud,
as if they sense a storm.

THE HANDS

I

When we overwhelm a village,
I am told to make sure
none will ever pull a trigger.

I go in with a machete,
come out with a sack of hands.
My fathers feed me, count the pairs.

In the darkness I feel cool
palms crawl up to stroke
my head, soft hairless

hand-backs on my cheeks.
Thumbs draw down my eyelids,
fingers shush my lips.

II

In a terracotta jar,
a tobacco-brown plant,
tight as a mummified fist.

*'Leave it in the rain,
and see what happens.'*
So we tipped it in the sink.

Amid the crockery
it unfurled and began to beg:
ever open, plaintive.

We kept it watered,
then, sick of supplication –
left it in the sun to clench.

JAIRUS

So, God takes your child by the hand
and pulls her from her deathbed.
He says: 'Feed her, she is ravenous.'

You give her fruits with thick hides
– pomegranate, cantaloupe –
food with weight, to keep her here.

You hope that if she eats enough
the light and dust and love
which weave the matrix of her body

will not fray, nor wear so thin
that morning sun breaks through her,
shadowless, complete.

Somehow this reanimation
has cut sharp the fear of death,
the shock of presence. Feed her

roast lamb, egg, unleavened bread:
forget the herbs, she has an aching
fast to break. Sit by her side,

split skins for her so she can gorge,
and notice how the dawn
draws colour to her just-kissed face.

GROUNDED

I

At the edge of sleep,
my head on your breast,
I hear your heart lock
with the cloth pulse

of a skein of geese,
which arrows over roofs
towards the source
of water, dreams, oblivion.

II

Asleep on your front,
your shoulder-blades reveal
themselves as wing-stumps.

Now I know what you
have given up for me,
for this November night,

this moonlit bed,
this sluicing rain
these distant fireworks.

And I think of migrants
on the wing for weeks,
filleting the air with sleep.

III

Today huge tethered kites
– torsos, mermaids, lizards, bears –
were animated by sea air,
as though the next world hung
above us like a mezzanine.

Tonight I lie awake and run
your absence through my fingers:
here's the touch of you,
your warmth and give,
our conspiracy of flightlessness.

CARNIVOROUS – II

The cook said: *'This lamb is for*
those who gave their lives for others.'

So the martyrs took the lamb.
It tasted rich, steeped in essence
of anchovy. They picked it clean
and found within, a goose, its pink
beak in the lamb's mouth like a tongue.

FLESH

At night the earth's flesh shifts,
which makes the house sigh
in its sleep, which sends a shiver

through the wood-bones of my bed,
which makes me stand up
in my dream and climb a hillside

flush with gorse and may.
I lie down on the peak and feel
the *kick-punch-kick*,

and wonder what the world's
child will be like – a newborn
island, steaming

with its own volcanic power,
violent and beautiful,
with empty orange skies

and seas too hot for fish,
a land of black dust raked
by iridescent fans of flightless birds,

fighting over unclaimed ground,
breaking in their voices with cacophonies
of courtship and alarm.

Morning comes, but no news
of a birth, no new islands
in the archipelago.

The world's child is lost amongst us,
unversed in our languages,
walking the streets with a bowl.

YOUR EYES TONIGHT

What does the moon say, for the role
it plays in this? Stars

sing through the back-cloth,
but the moon remains an orb of silence.

Such is its vacuum it has sucked in
all the unsaid, all the reticence,

lost words of peace, swallowed apologies.
It sets them into lead and tin

– not silver – to make a pewter zero,
voiceless O. It is a corpse. It is a seed too,

with all those words laid down
in seams within its core. If we keep

no secrets from each other, leave no
thoughts unuttered, then it cannot grow.

As if. These days, it shows at noon
above the roofscapes, bloated,

saying nothing, which is not to say
not saying things, but mouthing

nothing clear and full of meaning,
as a mantra or a name.

CARNIVOROUS – III

The cook said: *'Are there any here*
who spent their lives in flight?'

The exiles stepped up then, and tore
the goose apart. They turned it upside-down
to pluck the soft meat from its breast
and found a salmon coiled inside,
sealed in a crust of salt.

CHOREOGRAPHY

His fist smashes my face.
That's no wrestler's move;
so it's bare knuckles now. Okay.

There's blood in my eye,
the lid swells to a hood.
I use my head and butt him.

His lips bloom like a rose,
but he's still ticking, clicking
his tongue on the roof of his mouth.

Gamesmanship: the harder
I hit, the louder he clicks.
We raise the stakes:

he jabs me on the nose
to get my hands up,
then with otherworldly speed

he lands a right hand in my guts.
Agony: I'm folded,
dumbstruck, gasping like a fish.

He backs off a moment,
then he knees me in the jaw.
My teeth split the tip of my tongue.

I'm spitting now, incensed.
I grab two fistfuls of his shirt,
swing my foot behind his legs.

Shove. He staggers, falls
with me on top of him.
We've landed in the Jabbok creek.

I dunk his face to cool him off,
to make him choke and talk.
He comes up clicking still;

I slap him. He stares at me.
Are angels speechless? This one's
wingless, solid without weight.

Perhaps he's trying to talk?
It could be '*t*' or '*c*': some stammering
Gabriel with a message?

I relax my grip to listen,
he sees his chance and turns us,
rolls me in the stream,

taps the hollow of my thigh,
and something gives. He helps
me up. He's damaged me.

Somehow he's slid my hip
out of its bone-cup, left me
clipped and limping.

When I stand, his clicking stops.
It dawns on me: that was no stutter,
but a beat. The dance is over.

'You had me there', he says,
'I had to do your leg to settle things.'
He brushes off his shirt,

I hobble to the water's edge to wash.
I shout to him *'What was your name?'*
I don't know if he hears me.

THE RAZOR

His children heard the well-oiled
bees-buzz, found him
carpeting the house with hair.

His head was grey with scalp.
A ritual like that must mark
an end, or a beginning.

He washed his skull clean in the rain,
then – without turning – walked.
He left to climb a mountain,

he left to fight a cause –
to overthrow, to liberate, to cleanse,
to join a silent order.

He left because a huge dog leapt
at him, and struck him dumb;
at least, so said his wife.

Years went by. They gave him up.
His children wove his hair
with theirs and told him as a story.

MAPPING THE GENOME

Geneticist as driver, down the gene
codes in, let's say, a topless coupé
and you keep expecting bends,

real tyre-testers on tight
mountain passes, but instead it's dead
straight, highway as runway,

helix unravelled as vista,
as vanishing point. Keep your foot
down. This is a finite desert.

You move too fast to read it:
the order of the rocks, the cacti,
roadside weeds, a blur to you.

Every hour or so, you glimpse a shack
which passes for a motel here:
tidy faded rooms with TVs on

for company, the owner pacing out
his empty parking lot. And after
each motel you hit a sandstorm

thick as fog, but agony.
Somewhere out there are remnants
of our evolution, genes for how

to fly south, sense a storm,
hunt at night, how to harden
your flesh into hide or scales.

These are the miles of dead code.
Every desert has them.
You are on a mission to discover

why the human heart still slows
when divers break the surface,
why mermaids still swim in our dreams.

CARNIVOROUS – IV

The cook said: *'Come and eat if you
remember well the salt of tears.'*

So those who knew that taste too well
unwound the salmon's curl
and stripped the lukewarm flesh.
Stuck in its throat they found
a shell–less snail, fattened on milk.

THE DRIFTER AND
HIS WHITE SHADOW

I

Yes, the white shadow.
Sounds like a super-hero,
looks like an absence,
smells brackish, of mussel husks.
I struggle for more detail.

II

I sleep on the beach,
at the cutting-edge where blades
of star and ocean
whet against a belt of sand.
Night by night it sharpens me.

III

No matter how dark
my coat, how wide-brimmed my hat,
I print a blank shape.
My heels bruise the salt-drenched shore,
but sun gapes steely through me.

IV

White is not absence,
but an over-abundance,
colours on colours.
A shadow is not semblance,
more source, more maker's study.

Is it my own death,
stalking me, obsessed with me,
rehearsing the chalk
outline of my corpse? If so,
I do admire its patience.

VI

Is it a shadow
on an x-ray, elvers in
the alveoli,
swimming upstream to my mouth,
coughing out my final words?

VII

Or is it my form,
see-through, gentle, soul on strand,
at home in its skin?
It plays like a child, safe, sound,
I could watch it all day long.

VIII

I live on seafood.
My shadow lives on thin air.
No hound of heaven
chasing me down days and nights,
just a stray cur at my heels.

IX

We are related,
flesh-ghost. There is a purpose
in your hounding me.
Maybe one day I'll turn tail
and follow you, in silence.

X

I try to drown you,
drag you out into the waves,
but you come clearer,
even as your face is slit
by coral, as your throat floods.

XI

Genes of sand, these grains
are rummaged by the backwash.
They could turn ocean,
or may chance upon the codes
for ice-fields, mountains, forests.

XII

My shadow's gene-map
is identical to mine.
We are siamese,
joined at the feet, each of us
dependent on our soles' welt.

XIII

Summer, and shadows
sardine the beaches. My scared
albino brother
disappears all afternoon.
We meet again at low tide.

XIV

Walking the tide-line,
You try to link arms, hold hands.
Foam clings to driftwood,
bottles (no messages), weed.
Back off. I barely know you.

MADAME ZERO

Apples would turn waxy,
then waste as she handled them:

scarlet one bite, pink the next,
then she bit her fingers.

An anti-Midas, she began
to mistrust touch, the way

her stroke could snuff the gentle
light behind a cat's eyes,

how cigarettes burnt backwards,
ending in a puff of smoke.

She could make the world primeval,
pre-material, push it back

into the mind of God.
She took to wearing kid gloves,

but they vanished within minutes.
Rough hide mountain mitts

took half an hour to melt.
She bound her hands with bandages

as thick as boxing gloves,
but nothing could protect

the world from her caress.
When the gift turned inwards,

her blood began to turn to chalk,
her heart withdrew into its beat.

She walked the city streets all night,
kissing strangers,

then stood in an empty park
and reached to touch the sky itself.

CARNIVOROUS – V

'Has anyone here never hungered,
never run, never lost, never cried?'

The cook held the snail on a fork.
No-one replied, so he swallowed it.
Later, rumours spread that one man
slipped away, out into the driving rain,
leaving a clean plate in his place.

TO JOHN DONNE

Unlike an area of land, when you patent a gene,
you are enclosing a part of me, the shared landscape.
                                    Sir John Sulston

Now, as your mistress strips for bed,
her body is already mapped,
its ancient names a cracked code.

That new found land is paced out,
sized up, written down as hope
or prophecy, probability or doubt.

Her charts are held on laptops,
mastered by medics, laid bare.
Her peaks and gorges, fell slopes,

oceans, woodlands, stars,
this atlas of her is no mystic book,
it is a textbook of disease.

The sun turns dust to smoke,
and picks out, as it sets,
a path your hands might take

– your roving hands – she lets
them roam, though she's no landowner.
By law, her breast's

curve has a patent, so you know
that bankers – tired of gold –
have bought a piece of her and you.

You call her your America – too right.
Her wilderness, those prairies
have been carved up into real estate,

ranches ringed with barbed wire,
lights and guns. KEEP OUT
OUR DOGS EAT TRESPASSERS.

Do you care? Does she? What
can it matter at this fleet May dusk,
as you seek each other out,

and her body's secret name is much
like yours, and yours is so close
to the crab apple and silver birch

which interweave with collar doves
and greenfinches, akin to grass
which drapes in blossom as the light dies.

Let your hands, and hers, lead us
in love's mass trespass, let your lips,
and hers, claim back with whispers

the co-ordinates of bodies: TTA,
GAG, TGT, CCC, ATC, TGT (*this is,*
yes, a litany) CTG, GAG, TTG . . .

WHAT DIVIDES US

I

Skin is border country.
Ever exiled from each other,
we come here to meet.

In these edgelands, dusklands,
open but uncrossable,
we use a common tongue.

II

Since the word *skin* shares a root
– through Breton, Irish, Welsh – with *scale*,

and since in certain lights your back's
pale honey flashes silver,

since you swim so well, so fast,
forgive me if at night my hands

feel for vestigial fins and gills,
my fingers turn to hooks.

III

The mermaid's husband hid
her scale-suit, folded
in the coal-shed, black on black.

She knew, and kept it oiled
and salted. She saw it sometimes
as her past, sometimes her future.

IV

Back late, I leave a slumped
self-portrait on the chair,
a splayed corpse, limbs akimbo.

If I believed the soul
was separate from the body,
I might describe myself

as the soul of my clothes,
cut loose in an unlit afterlife
beneath a massive canopy of night.

My threads are guardians,
vigil-keepers at the bedside,
sleeping on the job.

In the half-light, they show
me hopelessly drunk, shot
through the heart, or drowned.

They are my boneless likeness,
a lightning conductor,
decoy for bad dreams.

V

Weavers strained to conjure this,
the ultimate pashmina:

wide enough to wrap his house,
fine enough to thread his wedding ring,

until *that is* his stitched initials snagged
and stopped it passing through.

The men they silenced
– now heads of tables –
slit their stitched lips free
as if to kiss and bless
the dinner knives.
They whisper grace
through open wounds.

GENETICS

In glass tanks under hot lights,
fruit flies tend the dark and pursing
wounds of apples, damsons,
in their watched wild gardens.

Drosophila melanogaster:
– Black–Bellied Honey-Lover –
heredity in hourly generations,
parenthood as fierce thirst for the future.

From their frantic pass–it–on
we learn that claret eyes
are paired with short straight wings,
sepia with long and curled.

From their urgent evolution,
fruit flies learn that days are long,
and suns are hot, and every garden
is abandoned in the end.

EDGE OF THE WORLD

Sand in the gale at low tide
like smoke with a sting,

and under it – half disinterred –
gold-scarlet razor shells,
like countless open coffins.

Their risen bodies – lissom,
made of light alone –
now burnish ribs of waves.

Gull and gannet shadows try
to take them (since they need
the light), but real birds

pull them back ashore
to pick at the cadavers.

MENAGERIE

I

Shut-eyed at a mirror,
she dabs her lids white
with kaolin and water.
By touch alone, she paints
her closed eyes open,
colourless and empty,
ghost-moths at a lantern.

II

Flashes on cheekbones,
white tiger war-paint,
lips drawn back from teeth.
Hush falls in Siberian forests.

III

Chin and lips next.
This camouflage allows
anonymity among the dead.
An arctic hare roots
for taint under snow.

IV

Brow to hairline now.
This make-up is a cure for age;
not in its density of clay,
but in its charge of water,
fresh from wounds
of ice-cracked mountains,

endlessly plural.
A rare animal of light,
she is too quick for death.

V

Neck, jaw–line, nose,
the mask almost complete.
She is an owl glimpsed
by flashlight in the tundra
above tree and snow lines,
a face from the past,
a print in the permafrost.

VI

Finished, a blushless,
bloodless head. As clay dries it
becomes a porcelain chrysalis,
she a locked-in crimson
silk moth in the making.

VII

Her mirror is a millpond.
Each day its white fish surfaces.

Cautious and clean-shaven
all his life, the next world
woke him gaunt and stubbled
by the shrinkage of his skin.

He turned down the banquet
– broth to brie – *'Later, later'*,
and went straight for the cigarettes.
'Do you have any with filters?'

STUDY FOR THE WORLD'S BODY

after the painting by RB Kitaj.

It only looks like an embrace
when frozen. In truth it is

a dance; unaccompanied and slow.
This house feels abandoned. How

a couple came to be here in an upstairs
room (nothing through the glass

but open sky), is immaterial.
The point is, they cannot tell

what has interrupted them,
some sound outside their room

has made him jump and swivel:
perhaps a weightless footfall,

a ventriloquist's trick, a voice
thrown, a voice cut loose

and trapped in its own simple
utterance. The stripped walls

of this house have made an aural
hall of mirrors, so a single

board creak is a possible epiphany,
each draught is a litany

of hopes and fears. What is it
he is so afraid of? She is not:

her white owl face is lineless,
eyes calm, lips apart but silent.

Her hand, on his shoulder still,
pulls him gently back, pulls

him back into the real world
of bodies in motion, the weight

and measure of a dance.
Here is a story of love, loss, chance,

not in the blank sky, sanded
boards, the coatless hanger

on a nail, the empty hanging
socket in each ceiling;

but among the perfect geometry
of unfurnished rooms, an intimacy

takes two people by surprise.
It may be, in the world's eyes

they should not be here,
but without their risk the house is bare.

HIDE

Water. Streets are coated,
flat roofs sag. There has been
a great spillage, a night-long
letting-go. A fat dog stands
foursquare in the road,
hypnotised by rain
and car horns.

We were lost last night,
between the shutter slats
and curtain's swell. The sap
of each of us – our electricity –
escaped among the vixen cries,
the cherry trees'
black blossom.

Now your voice is thinner,
and you listen for the missing
notes in mine. Your skin
is stripped of conductivity, as dead
as silk. Behind your eyes
lie memories learnt by heart.
We have gone,

but in our place are replicas,
exact in every blemish.
We begin to act the day.
It is understood that since
our simulacra are so perfect,
we will go on as if
nothing changed.

TONGUE

The strength that hid in silence,
that roped me in my sleep,

that gripped me on the gravel path
afraid to carry on in case

my own steps masked the steps
of an assassin; that strength

in stillness, that warm bone,
that iron bar, that held-breath power

has broken into speech, in tongues
I cannot understand. Tables talk

to windows, twisted hazel hisses
at the ring-mesh fence behind it.

Brush a poppy-head and hear
it curse you, spitting seeds

across its own sealed mouth.
Cats at night are drowned out

by the carcasses in bins,
and by the stars themselves,

as deafening as sirens.
Walls hold traces of old words

among their horsehair, plaster, lime.
Even people talk now,

knocking out a morse code on
the walls between their cells.

What separates them is their
only means of contact.

PATHOLOGIST

Autopsy means *'to see with one's
own eyes'*. I have seen too much.
I strip away all evidence of health:

perfect livers pale as sand at ebb tide,
lungs light and intricate as coral,
kidneys like soft turtles' eggs,

and worst of all, the hearts
– so fresh – lukewarm and shimmering,
resonant with sudden stillness.

I eviscerate, then fill the cavity
with seawashed pebbles, just enough
to bring the dead weight back.

In my dreams they wake,
bend aside the roots which stitched
them underground, and stagger,

spitting out my stones as if
still spellbound by the flavour
of the fruit which held such seeds.

THE GIFTS

Caspar, Balthazar, Melchior,
your wisdom contracted
to a single pinpoint star.

Your gifts – you may have guessed –
were abandoned when
the ingrate family left.

Not wanting their boy
to be rich, priestly, dead,
they took the empty boxes.

Your gold, Caspar, essence
of bees' souls, fossil honey
sifted out of streams,

was found dumped at a tree's
forked root. Some was burnt
and beaten into leaf,

to line the windows of stretch
limos, to gild great statues
tarnished by the rain.

Some was eaten
as an antidote to death,
but just broke teeth.

Balthazar, your incense,
frank and pure, mistaken for
a cache of spider's eggs,

was left to hatch until
a stray dog caught the scent
and dug it up.

They ground it into fragrance
to mask the stench of blood
on battlefields,

to calm the nerves
on death row,
to steady trigger-fingers.

Melchior, the myrrh,
dark undertaker's oil,
what kind of gift was that

to bless a newborn? No
surprise she gave it
to the first who asked –

an old, arthritic shepherd,
who rubbed it on his back
until his bed smelt like a tomb.

When you got home,
did you strip your palaces
and walk the hills alone?

Was the boy's cry with you?
or did his silence echo out
from the manger

to the town walls strafed
with bullets, from falling bells
with severed ropes

to quiet cells
and shanty towns where
one child wakes a city.

Did his absence
keep you sleepless
– flat out on the frost –

waiting for your eyes
to find a trace in
the utter starlessness?

Or did you keep the memory
of the breath of that child
on the back of your hand,

a whisper on the skin
that somehow grew stronger
and closer than bone.

A WRECK

Of starfish on a shingle beach,
rare catch by the March wind.

Countless five-toothed cogs mesh
as a powerless machine. Dead

and dying are irreconcilable.
Once the ghost is given up, they dry

to ornaments, inanimate as shells.
In our vanishing bright future,

human hearts will be like these
tight windmills with a carapace.

Pillowed on a chest, one lover
may tease the other's turbine

hum out of the streetlight's
buzz and voltage of the house.

Death will be a pulled plug,
five blades slowing to a cold star.

Selected out: the frailty of flesh,
vicissitudes of rhythm.

Never a true source of passion,
heart will then mean *equilibrium*.

THE FREQUENCY

This could be an explanation:
why we hear trees as wash and sibilance,
but swallows hear one thread
of a polyphony, an invitation.

Does the dusk call them down,
or vice versa? Plumping on wires like
ripe fruit, bluebirds darken into blackbirds,
and their talk weighs heavy

as the air swells with water. Even
the first rain has a voice as it begins its fall,
long before it breaks across
radio masts, roof gardens, cairns.

It strikes a note too high for us,
though animals with sharper ears
do look up at the song, and lean for cover.
You're a prisoner of rhythm.

I believe that. Night falls now,
and under lightlessness I listen
for the footfalls of God in the garden.
The cool of evening is the time

he walked beneath the boughs of Eden,
softly, with his lips dried shut.
The apple was gone, man and woman
with it, and already

the bass tones of birdsong
were becoming shrill, sonorities
of breeze in grass were turning
into whispers. This was the fall of sound,

a rise in frequency, which rendered paradise
inaudible. An army
of recordists could remind us what we lost,
could tape and slow by half,

then half again, then half, until we hear
the moans of distant suns like whalesong,
until human voices slow to growls
and ratchet to a standstill.

Then — *shock* — our own breath,
when its pitch is slowed contains
the uncensored language of the heart,
yes words, our every sigh gives us away.

FOOD FOR RISEN BODIES – VI

Abeja blanca zumbas – ebria de miel – en mi alma.
Pablo Neruda

No longer ravenous, they smoke
and sip. Some carry tables out

to get a feel for sun on skin again.
More words are coming back,

so there's a lot of naming.
Old ones still hold good – *oak,*

brook, crab, sycamore – but more
are needed now. They mull

potential titles for these new
white bees, as sharp as stars

against the ivories of cherry
or magnolia. Word gets round

the bees were new creations
made in honour of a poet,

so they wait for him to choose.
He's in no hurry, cups them

in his hands, weighs up the tenor
of their hum. The sun brings colour

to the diners' sallow skins.
Although these bodies were not

theirs before, there are resemblances,
and flesh retains a memory

even beyond death, so every
lover's touch, each blow or cut

is rendered into echo on the hand,
the lips, the neck. Some fall silent,

while their own phenomenology
is mapped across them.

Others look astonished,
expecting their new skin to be

a blank sheet, but the man
who went ahead to find a route

for them came back with wounds
intact and palpable. No pain,

but a record nonetheless, a history
of love and war in blank tattoos.

COSMOLOGY

Hold tight, for the world
is at full tilt tonight,
clocks cannot keep pace.

Solar systems scream asunder,
star clouds are a powder blast
of ancient light.

Hold fast to me, because
the universe is one long
shrapnel burst, out and away

from the heart. Up there,
the only contacts are collisions
of stars as they fly apart.

Or maybe stars are still,
like us, and it's the space
between them which explodes.

LAST THINGS

for Ruth

Before we swim, your earrings
are the last things to be taken off,
like rare shells turned for centuries
by hands beneath the waves.

On heaps of clothes their clasps
could catch birds as they catch the light,
could tempt, hook and reel them in
from sand-bars and islets.

With two lobe-holes like birthmarks,
you are open to the water's touch,
though salt will try to heal you
of this greater nakedness.

NATAL

Sick of being tailed by death,
I searched for my beginnings.

I wandered on the ice-floes,
at the Poles, in hope of something

pearl-like, some warm winter seed
with a striated core of ice.

All I found were faults and fissures.
So I hunted close to home,

in the eyes of my children,
in the purse-lipped pockets of my heart.

I felt like giving up the quest,
saying *yes* to the white-suited stalker,

who leans in doorways, smoking,
catches my eye with no enmity,

whose smile says: *'I can wait.'*
But I shook him off, and traced my birth

back to a café in the tropics.
She (why hadn't I expected that?)

was sipping sweet clear liquor
on a wide Sargasso harbour-front.

She smelt of coconut. She wore dark
blue; formal, almost sombre.

She stripped green olives with her teeth
and threw the stones into the sea.

I wanted to apologise, but could not
remember who abandoned who.

ANATOMY OF A PERFECT DIVE

I

The sill is peppering with storm-flies.
Colours deepen. *Too close.* Time to change.

Shed your clothes like pointless wings.
Now it's just the weight of you.

Rocks, sun, waves have kept a place for you.
Expecting guests? No matter. *Go.*

II

Feet on the brink. Avoid brushing earth
from your soles. Some trace of it

can cross the border with you:
flecks of other people on your skin and hair,

their wounds in your scars.
Their memories? The ones they told you.

III

Look down. *Don't.* It's up to you.
If you can treat the view as abstract, then

IV

reach up with your arms, as if this was
less dive, more surrender,

less surrender, more ascension. Stretch
until your heels lift from the sandstone.

V

Or, depending on the kind of dive,
point your arms straight forward, like

a sleepwalker, a ghost without a sheet.
Think of it as blind–man's–buff with eyes.

Your *risk-taker* gene tussles with your
terra-firma gene. Ignore them.

VI

Unlock your knees. Fear is normal.
Let them hinge and hold. Trust them,

VII

they'll kick when the time comes.
Remember, your ancestors were fish.

You'll be surprised what you remember.
Lean in. Tilt from the top until

VIII

your weight, your body, *you*, pulls you
through the frame like a defenestration.

IX

You've left the world. *There*. The land
was thin. The land, *let's be honest*, was dying.

X

Technically, this is the crux.
You are living a half-life between

two elements. You may wish at this stage
to be photographed or painted.

Now you know what your solidity is for:
so gravity has something to work with.

XI

Like a Rose of Jericho, you open,
flourish, but the rose needs saturation.

You just need a thought of sea.
Yes, you uncurl like yourself in the arms

of the midwife, stretching to test
the bounds, *there are none*, to fill the space.

XII

At the apex, some will say you hit
a perfect pitch: earth, air,

body, in an equilibrium as delicate
as *say* Piero's 'Baptism' –

poise, golden section, a circle
of utter concentration.

XIII

Some see in your dive the future,
see the universe expanding

to a point of grace and balance,
then holding that forever in fulfilment,

the cacophony of spheres gathered
to a final chord without decay.

XIV

The diver drops. The universe continues
ever out *for now* in search of harmony.

XV

To you, this trip from land to water
is as good as instantaneous, a finger snap.

But as you shape to cut the surface,
light has beaten you *as ever* to it.

XVI

This is diving, not dying. The next
move matters. Give the ocean (let's say

it's a high cliff leap) your fingertips.
Make offerings of them. No need

to worry about arms, head, torso, legs.
The sea will weave its fingers into

yours, and pull you to its heart
at irresistible speed.

XVII

So touch is first to break the blue,
then you get the stench of salt, weed, fish.

XVIII

Eyes adjust to a cerulean world
of blurred shapes, shades of silt.

XIX

As for ears, they drown in a domain
which sounds like the inner ear itself.

XX

Sheer momentum drives you deep.
What if the terminal velocity

of stars is so great that they lose
their equilibrium as soon as find it,

on, on, on, an endless vanishing,
until suns are so distant from planets

that life is wintered out? *Whatever.* You
bend, arch, brake. Dive becomes swim.

XXI

Atavistic skills kick in now: pulse slows,
eyes glaze; webbing opens fingers, toes.

XXII

You begin to melt, head first,
hair diffusing, clear lines of your form

dissolving. But you gain slow-motion.
Everyone looks graceful underwater.

XXIII

Out in the nick of time, the strong sun
reconstitutes you. *Back*. Round your mouth,

a lick of salt. At home, casement
windows bang. Net curtains haunt the rooms.

Your visitors stand in their coats,
looking for a note, a trace of you.